Time is the grist mill of the Universe.

time
time
time
time
time
time
time
time
time
time
time
time
time
time
time
time
time
time
time
time
time
time
time
time
time
time
time
time
time
time
time
time
time
time
time
time
time
time
time
time
time
time
time
time
time
time
time
time
time
time
time
time
time
time

time
time
time
time
time
time
time
time
time
time
time
time
time
time
time
time
time
time
time
time
time
time
time
time
time
time
time
time
time
time
time
time
time
time
time
time
time
time
time
time
time
time
time
time
time
time
time
time
time
time
time
time
time
time
time
time
time
time
time
time
time
time
time
time
time
time

It's a Matter of Time

a personal statement in verse and picture

by

Lester D. Roark

Time is a scavenger of broken threads,

and a weaver of bright new dreams.

Time is fresh footprints on a sandy beach,

and the stroking trowel of the water's edge.

Carolina Heritage Press
Lester D. Roark
P.O. Box 669
Shelby, North Carolina 28150

(initial publication)

Library of Congress cataloging in publication data.

Printed in the United States of America.

Contents

Time is the scrap heaps of Winter,

and the greening fields of Springtime.

time
time
time
time
time
time
time
time
time
time
time
time
time
time
time
time
time
time
time
time
time
time
time
time
time
time
time
time
time
time
time
time
time
time
time
time
time
time
time
time
time
time
time
time
time
time
time
time
time
time
time
time
time
tin

Preface

Premeditatedly, this is a book of questions, not answers.

What is Time?

Where did it come from?

When, if ever, did it begin?

When, if ever, will it end?

Herein, you will find nothing remotely resembling an answer to these or any other questions dealing with the immeasurable dimensions of Time itself.

This book is not offered as a resource of facts or scientific discoveries. It is not a debate with Einstein, Darwin, or Bronowski. It is not an attempt to write another version of the Bible or to offer new interpretations of previous versions.

It is, purely and simply, a philosophical statement and, therefore, personal. It is a product of the process of reading and writing and quietly observing human responses to the movement of Time and Time's impact on all THINGS -- past, present and future. These wandering thoughts came into sharper focus after long hours of conversation with dear friends and acquaintances who shared a level of patience, provocativeness and mental agility to give us -- occasionally -- the heady notion that we had, indeed, found the answer.

 (This book acknowledges the subsequent and sobering reality that such was not the case.)

Consequentially, this book was produced for the quiet pleasure of writing and to satisfy a personal desire to share these thoughts, observations and impressions of a lifetime -- some jotted on now-yellowing bits of paper and others long moored in the harbor of my mind.

It is my hope that you, from whatever mental resources you apply, will gain a sense of joy and wonderment as you read this book and, more importantly, that you will come to fully enjoy and more deeply appreciate your own brief period of Experienced Time.

-- The Author

Time is the casting of seeds, and a harvest of grain.

…some Special Words…

with special thanks
to wife, Dot,
and children, Pam and Jeff,
for giving me Time.

dedicated,
with deep appreciation, to
Ed Hamrick, my high school English teacher,
who encouraged me, fifty one years ago,
to become a writer of books.
His friendship and his counsel
have been warm and genuine
for half a century, now.
I trust that he will give a better grade
on the Quality of this offering,
than the grade already recorded
for the timetable I used in producing it.

to the late John W. Elliott, Sr.,
dear friend, who admonished me
repeatedly for thirty years, or more:
"Dammit, get that down on paper."

to Jim White, longtime friend,
who opened the door to my first job
as a writer in 1952;
who introduced me, in 1955, to the lady
who became my wife in 1956;
and, who gave me his good
second-hand computer in 1990
and showed me how to use it.

and, warmly,
to all who have been
circumstantially hindered
in claiming Time as a friend.

Time . . . the Beginning . . . ? . . . ? . . . ? . . . .

Not by a Timer's hand,
Pressing a stopwatch button;

Not at the flash
Of some Big Bang;

Not with the sucking of Matter
Into a Black Hole in Space.

Time Was, in fact . . .

Brooding in the darkness
Of that vast void;

Waiting while architects of the Universe
Were yet in their sterile wombs;

Watching through all eternities past
While Space and Matter assembled.

Time Was
And Is
And Will Be . . .

Only a silent observer
Standing at an open door;

Only a permissive witness
Allowing all things to happen,

Even all things that have been,
And all things that are yet to be.

Time is Eternity Past,
Its Beginning Never Was . . . .

Time: Its Own Miracle

Omnipresent: *om-ni-pres-ent | adj :*
    "present in all places,
    present at all times."

Time is indeed omnipresent,
    time is the oldest "nothing,"
    time is its own miracle.

Time is as young as it ever was.

Time is as old as it will ever be.

Time has no gears of pace or speed,
    time is a constant.

The young and old grow older together,
    animate and inanimate,
    ageing by the same calendar.

The sleeping baby on mother's lap,
    grows older by the minute,
    as does the mother.

The gnarled, thunderstruck and dying tree,
    grows older at a pace in time,
    as does a green and sprouting acorn.

Time: Forever A Question

Time is a strident messenger,
    a patient listener;

Time says all it needs to say,
    receives all it wishes to hear;

Time's voice is the song of a mockingbird,
    and rumbling roar of thunder;

Time's ear can hear the clouds float by,
    and silence of a baby's slumber;

Time's eye can see the Summer winds,
    and fragrance of Springtime flowers;

Time is contained only by itself,
    and roams a range that has no boundary.

Yesterday's Flower

Time's flower fresh blooming on yesterday,
      was full of fragrance,
      the silken tenderness of Youth,
      was admired by lovers who strolled the path,
      and caressed by bees that sucked its nectar.

Time is yesterday's flower today,
      withered, neglected, and fallen prone
      upon the path of cobblestone,
      where unmindful lovers trample it underfoot,
      and bees seek out new fresh blossoms.

Time And Beauty

Time gives time for beauty.

      from soaring snow-crowned mountains
      to gentle hills of dogwood blooms;

      from thunder of crashing waterfalls
      to gentle streams that play their trickle music;

      beyond the awe and mystery of mighty canyons
      to the quiet and narrow cove at journey's end.

Time gives time to nurture our souls.

      beauty is for our time to look and see,
      there are paths to guide us, the view is free.

              scuffy autumn leaves,
            green moss on river banks,
     wild winds and shifting sands along the dunes,
           dead trees and rotting stumps,
             and hyacinths a'bloom . . .
              all have measured days,
                but endless cycles.

Time is a rotting stump, and a sprouting acorn.

Somewhere. Time

It is Springtime, somewhere.

    Birds make music

    with their nesting chores,

    and worms wiggle

    in the warming wood.

Somewhere, in Time,

    early blossoms wave

    sweet-scented heads,

    and eager sprouts seek out

    a touch of sunshine.

                Fresh waters splash and trickle

                  around fast darting minnows,

               the hound peels back a heavy lid

             and yawns away the nights of Winter.

In Springtime, somewhere, lovers walk

    with hands entwined

    and hearts in focus,

    while crickets chirp their serenade

    and drape-clouds dim the prying moonbeams.

Somewhere in Time, somewhere in Space,

    there comes the hour, there looms the place,

    of when and where the magic stroke is cast,

    to seize the hour and claim our spot at last.

Time Ain't Got No Handle

"You know, Mister John,"

    an old black man said,

"Time ain't go no handle on it,

    you just have to get a-hold of it

    the best way you can."

    His white man friend listened.

"That don't let you 'rastle with it too much," he added.

    "And, Lord knows,

    you can't do much

    about hurryin' it up or slowin' it down."

    His friend was paying attention.

"No sir,

    I figure 'bout all a man can do

    is to just sit down

    and think about it."

    And, they did,

    for a long Time.

"In the still cadence of Time,

when the only sound is Silence,

I hang my soul on a dead tree limb,

and watch the sunlight through it . . ."

" ...I speak not of Things, but of Time itself."

The Beginning

"In The Beginning."

Genesis.

The first three words,

Of the first sentence,

In the very first chapter . . .

. . . "In The Beginning."

And thus, the path, the starting point.

      To probe the ultimates of Time,

      from Past to Present to Future,

      one is obliged, it seems,

      to commence with whatever it is

      that has been called "The Beginning."

Bewildering journey.

      Along the fuzzy edge of Space,

      in the dark caverns of Time,

      void of Light and Matter,

      there is but a maze of mental shadows,

      . . . and a gripping question:

        "How Long Ago?"

Does it matter, really?

> Not much, perhaps,
>
> except for Man's insatiable curiosity,
>
> delighted fascination,
>
> and mental stimulation,
>
> from wondering about the vast unknowns.

A joyous journey, indeed it is,

> to ponder such a mystery,
>
> while granted the certainty of knowing
>
> that answers will not come.

Questions without answers because of The Law!

> A Law, heretofore,
>
> perhaps, unwritten and unspoken,
>
> embracing Time and Space and Matter.

It holds, eternally, and quite simply:

> "Matter cannot exist
>
> without Space to accommodate it;
>
> Neither Matter nor Space can exist
>
> without the encompassing stretch of Time
>
> to embrace them,
>
> to measure them, and,
>
> to record their existence."

Time, alone.

 Time, per se, in and of itself,

 is unencumbered by darkness,

 unrestrained by an endless void

 and unimpressed by a Universe

 of Space and Matter.

Time is a cycle.

 Cycles are cycles,

 they come and go,

 the end of one,

 the beginning of another,

 and over again . . . they are perpetual.

Time, in sequential cycles,

 patient in its own shadow,

 observing the order of events,

 thus waited . . . is waiting . . . will wait.

Time, the eternal and vigilant witness,

 thus observed

 the Creation of all things,

 animate and inanimate,

 here and elsewhere.

Time, the endurable measuring rod,

    yet lingers patiently,

    to witness the destruction of all things,

    and all recurring cycles of new Creations,

    somewhere along the road to Eternity.

The Creation Story?

The Heavens and the Earth?

    Transitory events that hang suspended

    in the unmeasured canopy of Space

    and the limitless reaches of Time.

And, so it was!

    Time stood its silent vigil

    while matter, and form,

    and substance, and light,

    and all the building blocks of the Universe

    were floating on yet uncharted courses.

Mental persistence, most likely,

    still propels that nagging question:

    "How Long Ago?"

If that be so, perchance,

    in one grand moment of discovery and humbleness,

one's mind will find exhilaration

flowing freely from the noble confession:

"I just don't know."

What?

 Surrender to benign conclusions?

Nay, not self-effacing;

Nay, not a statement

of intellectual stagnation or mediocrity;

No, it is not so!

'Tis but a grand and self-enriching response

to a question that has no answer,

singular, plural, or proven.

Time is not seen; Time is not heard;

Time does not occupy Space;

Time does not create Matter;

Time does not consume anything,

not even itself.

Time, simply, allowed and allows all things to happen;

Time was not created by other powers or forces;

Time was Past and Present and Future,

even before any other thing was created.

Time will continue,

even after all things, animate and inanimate,

have vanished from here, and elsewhere.

Time, illimitable, immeasurable,

before all things,

during all things,

after all things.

How Long Ago?

Time?? . . . . The Beginning Never Was. ❐

"…I speak of birth and death and Living Time."

Experienced Time

We live,

We breathe,

We have our being.

> Three score years and ten,
>
> or less,
>
> or more.

Experienced Time.

> Whatever span,
>
> from birth to death,
>
> is but a flash,
>
> a minuscule tracing,
>
> on Time's limitless chart.

In quiet, eternal patience,

> Time has sufficient measure
>
> to mark every breath
>
> and record every heartbeat.

Beyond these curtains of our stage,

> Time has the stretch and stricture
>
> to open the door for our coming
>
> and close the door when we take leave.

The Door opens.

A hospital ward, polished, sterile;

Time hangs on the cadence

of those who carry instruments of care

and capsules of comfort.

Time is measured and recorded

At a minute

Of an hour

In a day

Of a month

And a year.

A pregnant womb

gives up its infant passenger,

delivering a new being

upon the untended lap of Time.

Time was, and is, and will be, its enabler.

As Time enabled it to become what it now is,

Time will allow it to become what it is yet to be.

Time will be its hunger

and its fulfillment.

Time will be its alchemy of hope

and its wailings of despair.

Time will be its cries of joy

    and its tears of sorrow.

Time will be its shattered dreams

    and its bright new visions.

 Its dawn and dusk

    and its hours of midnight;

 Its scrap heaps of Winter;

    fresh blossoms of Springtime;

Its vigor of Youth;

    its frailty of Age.

Time is thus the hollow promise,

    but not the provider.

Time is the open door to a vacant span;

    we tip-toe through it,

    brushing with the good and bad,

    and touching hands with the cruel and the kind.

Time, always our silent witness,

    as we move along

    past fleeting scenes

    of sunrises and sunsets,

    past tears and laughter,

    sad songs and happy throbbings.

Time observes our grand parade,

      but speaks no words of praise;

      it sees each stumbling step,

      but speaks no words of scorn.

Time, the permissive sentinel,

      and patient by the open door,

      waits while we grasp at glory

      and tune our ears to praise,

      or stoop to lend a helping hand

      to a stranger along the way.

Time, encompassed in this brief span,

      sealed in the record books,

      from birth to death,

      is our Experienced Time.

Thus, Time, indeed,

      is the promise of a pregnant womb.

Long down another corridor,

      in a quiet room,

      Time is silent,

      Time is certain,

      Time is obedient to its unwritten disciplines.

The Door closes.

Time is measured and recorded

At a minute

Of an hour

In a day

Of a month

And a year.

Time will make its deposit,

returning it to the womb of Earth

in some appointed place

at some appointed Time.

Time, in full cycle, indeed becomes

the despair of a cold grey corpse.

Time thus resolves our destiny . . . in Time.

Time is

the coming, the going,

the giving, the taking

of Life.

Time, in its patient pace,

folds up the shroud

and wipes away the tears.

Thus, in the full body of Time,

>   beyond our own brief span

>   of Experienced Time,

>   there will be countless other spans,

>   ushered in on the cries of new beings;

>   ushered out on the muffled sobs of mourners.

Thus, Time, in its endless cycles,

>   with no gifts to give,

>   offers naught but blank pages

>   of eternal promise.

Time will not be too busy,

>   but move with patient certainty.

Time will have many things to do,

>   but will not grow weary.

Time has a span and a reach,

>   adequate for eternity's happenings.

Time, as a sterile vacuum,

>   creates nothing, destroys nothing.

Time, without weapon and without balm,

>   inflicts no injuries, provides no healing.

Time delivers without Invocation.

Time takes without Benediction.

Time Was, Time Is, Time Will Be.

Time, itself,

is the Boundary of Experienced Time. ❐

Time rakes up the pieces of broken promises.

Time is the birthplace of Expectation, and the cradle of Hope.

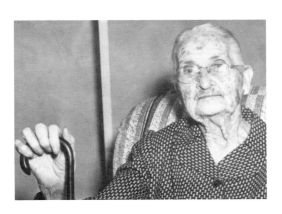

"…I speak only to the limit of one's imaginings."

Speculative Time

Speculative Time:

> Immeasurable spans
>
> stretching into an infinity
>
> on both ends
>
> of our one brief certainty.

Bewildering thought.

> Eternity Past,
>
> Eternity Future,
>
> transcending all circumstances
>
> of Eternity Present.

In our wonderment,

> we are as islands
>
> in a sea of Time,
>
> unable to probe
>
> beyond its horizon.

Beyond this, and all of this,

> beyond all we know, or claim to know,
>
> beyond conjecture, argument and debate,
>
> Time roamed and roams its boundless range.

Unharnessed Time,

       beyond our mental tethering rein,

       dimensions are shrouded in veils of mystery,

       focused only in fuzzy speculation.

Speculative Time.

       Speculation begets questions,

       questions beget questions,

       and answers do not come.

How long ago was claimed the starting point?

How far ahead the calculated stopping?

Speculation?

       Vain as it is, it is!

       And so?

       And so, we Contemplate.

       Contemplating both ends of Eternity

       by wondering about the Past

       and worrying about the Future.

Contemplations!

       Producing nothing more

       than fantasies

       and mesmerized amusements.

To wit and Twenty billion years, or so, ago,

> (that's 20 with nine naughts to follow),

> the experts say, or thereabouts,

> perhaps or maybe,

> our Universe

> came into being.

(The Experts, one should note,

> perhaps in fits of propitious discretion,

> parenthetically speaking,

> did not mention previous Universes!)

Alas, our present Universe, then,

> at the tender Age

> of fifteen billion years, they say,

> (it's only 15 now, but still nine naughts to follow),

> gave birth to Mother Earth,

> according to geologists.

Behold, the experts politely suggest:

> *"give or take*

> *one-half billion years or so."*

> (more simply stated, that's 500

> with only six naughts following).

(Oh, by the way,

      the experts declare,

      these are all numbers rounded.

      Presumably, then, square ones

      did not fit as well.)

The Earth, They say, first whirled

      as a dark and formless void.

      Then, sometime thereafter,

      light and water came,

      and things took shape.

Animate and inanimate things appeared,

      grasses grew,

      and fishes swam, and all the living things

      began to multiply.

Then, somewhere back in Time,

      a scant fifty million years, or so,

      according to Bronowski,

      a small, tree-dwelling creature,

      called a lemur,

      came along, and others contend,

      that it was destined from the start,

      to gain homo sapien status.

Well, at any rate, apparently,

it jumped into the midst of all creation,

giving birth to varied bits of speculation,

from which evolved a long-drawn argument.

Was it Creation in a flash?

Or Evolution yet in process?

Introduce the dimensions of Time,

and the twain could live in harmony.

Time, itself, asks all the questions:

Why?

And When?

And How?

Time, itself, has all the answers

to Speculative Time,

but will not tell, except to say:

"No matter now,

no matter the circumstances,

the comings and the goings,

no matter the actors,

the stage settings,

the properties,

the directors."

No matter Now or Then.

Time is but Time.

> Time has no beauty
>
> save images reflected;
>
> it has no virtue
>
> save everlasting patience;
>
> it has no power
>
> beyond that to endure.

Time, in its Eternal whirl of Things,

> is out of a Past too long ago to measure,
>
> into a Future too far ahead to comprehend.

Time was, it had to be,

> before the cornerstone was laid,
>
> beneath the wall of our Great Universe.

Time will be, it will have to be,

> after all the stones are bits of dust,
>
> blowing and drifting on eternal winds.

Time is the blending

> of the old day
>
> and the new day.

Time is a vast sky

> colored by the light of sunrises
>
> and the slanting shadows of sunsets.

Time is dawn and dusk

    and the darkness of midnight.

Time is the happy quandary

    of unknown to unknown,

    the mental cobwebs

    in Man's library

    of Speculative Time. ❏

Time is the flash of a lone firefly,

    and the light of a star's eternity.

Time is the vigor of Youth, and the frailty of Age.

"…I speak of Calendars, Clocks and old Gravestones."

Time's Measuring Devices

Time, itself.

    Time, and all of its calibrations,

    all of its measuring devices,

    its "Alpha" and its "Omega,"

    are mere contrivances of Man.

Indeed, the rhythm of Nature

    set some absolutes:

    the changing of the Seasons,

    the cycles of Sun and Moon,

    the certain rise and fall of Ocean Tide,

    that, in their steady turn, fell prey to measure.

But alas, 'twas Time's late-coming visitor/Man,

    in fits of mental hunger,

    who made the calculations,

    arranged the charts to accurate scale,

    then invented tools to measure.

Clocks with long, sweeping hands,

    and swinging pendulums,

    sound the ticking seconds of Time.

Clocks, with computerized numbers,

 in lighted, moving digits,

 flash pulse beat seconds of Time.

Sun dials and slanted shadows,

Hour glasses and the shifting sands,

A sounding knell from the village spire,

The long shrill whistle of the factory's call.

 Time's measuring devices,

 calibrated to minutes and hours,

 orchestrate the ordered rules

 of mechanized, and scheduled, humanity.

 Time's measuring devices,

 tangible instruments and visible,

 sufficiently accurate and reliable,

 command our attention and respect.

And, Time itself,

 beyond computed digitals and millisecond readings,

 Time has left some vaguer clues:

 like hieroglyphics on an ancient cavern wall,

 wooden logs of stone in the desert sands,

 old gravestones in a weed-infested yard,

 a river chisel carving on the Canyon floor.

Their times and dates are left in blank,

despite Man's search for certainty,

recorded on the quiet, untended list,

of "best estimates"

or, perhaps, an "educated guess."

Time is history.

History is a chronicle of events,

and people tend, perhaps in mental dalliance,

or in polite and proper deference,

to accept Time as simply that:

A Chronicle of Events.

Events.

Events, in the narrow span of Experienced Time,

are recorded in the range from birth to death,

with unknown days and numbers given,

all credits duly paid,

all debits clearly drawn.

Events.

Events, beyond our span of Time,

are given dates of year and month and day,

documented and certified as truth

by witness/writers at the scenes,

and spread across a page of history.

Events.

Events, beyond the range of Experienced Time,

and beyond the verities of recorded history,

are listed in the Catalog of Unanswered Questions:

"How Many Years?"

"How Long Ago?"

And thus,

the capsules of Time:

how vast or scant in days and years?

How bright or dark in joys and tears?

The capsules of Time:

how well will they withstand

abrasion of the elements?

how firm will hold their deeds

against the wagging tongues of history?

To track the measurable increments

of our Experienced Time,

we use schedules and diaries,

calendars and clocks;

then fractionalize our given years

to fit specifics of daily happenings.

To probe the unmeasured reach,

    beyond our kinship with self-claimed days and years,

    we Speculate, we bemuse ourselves,

    interpreting hieroglyphics on a cavern wall,

    wondering how old the petrified log might be,

    or seeking a wax-rubbed message

    from an old gravestone.

Beyond all we know, first hand,

    by sight or sound,

    by touch or smell or taste,

    beyond the mental garner of recorded history,

    beyond the ancient, dull-blunted measuring sticks

    of "best estimates" and "educated guesses,"

    beyond all of this . . . is Time.

TIME: The word is broadly used,

    according to dictionaries.

    Time: a period of history,

    a division of geologic chronology,

    a term of military service,

    a prison sentence,

    measurement for a prevailing condition,

    the recorded point at which an event occurs.

And, many more,

    according to Webster,

    including the gripping challenge:

    "Time….a continuum

    which lacks spatial dimensions

    and in which events

    succeed one another

    from past through present to future."

Time thus was moving

    while the log of stone

    was a young green tree

    growing in the forest.

Time thus will be moving

    when ancient gravestones

    are reduced to grains of sand

    shifting on the desert wind.

Time is Experienced.

Time is Speculative adventure.

Time is measured by Man's technology,

    while Time, itself, is beyond measure.

Time is a quandary of abstract dimensions.

Time.

Before.

Now.

After.

Time Will Be. ◻

Time is a boulder at the river's edge,

and grains of sand on an endless beach.

Time is the promise of a tender bud, and the gift of a flower's full bloom.

"…I speak of the Boundless and the Faceless."

Beyond Quantity and Without Quality

Quantity?

How much?

How much Time?

Time, itself, forever and alone,

Despite all human contradictions,

Escapes the snare of measured numbers.

It is Man and Man's penchant

For dates and happenings and facts,

And his mental adventures in wondrous speculation,

That compels the searching questions of measured time.

How many years, how long the time,

Since our Universe came into being?

How old its offspring Earth?

That long and winding river?

That craggy mountain side?

How many days will you be gone?

How many years was Grandpaw when he died?

How much time is it going to take?

Time, silent and invisible,

Asks no questions and gives no answers.

Time, free and eternal,

is unencumbered by cares,

unharnessed by plans or schedules.

Thus, in its quiet, eternal movement,

Time is unrestrained by measured Quantity,

Feeding only upon its undiminished self.

In that hush of everlasting solitude,

Time roams its boundless range,

Before all things, during all things, after all things.

Time was, and is, and will be,

Illimitable, immeasurable, racing, unbounded

By Man's imaginings of a Beginning and an End.

Quality?

How good?

How bad the Time?

Time, itself, forever and alone,

Despite all human pronouncements,

Has earned no grade on Quality's score card.

It is man and man's own zeal,

To gain the best and escape the worst,

That plants the label of Quality upon the face of Time.

"Did you have a good time at the beach?"

"Oh yes, I had a fantastic time."

"How are you faring in this recession?"

"I'm having a hard time making ends meet."

How good the time? How bad?

For better or for worse,

Time, invisible and silent, radiates no beauty,

sings no songs of joyous cheer,

inflicts no injuries and bears no scars.

Time, groomed only in its faceless self,

moves quietly on its sterile journey,

unadorned and unabused by measured Quality.

Yet, in its spread of endless arms,

Time has the reach to embrace it all:

    beauty and blemish,

    silken touch and callous hand,

    hyacinths in springtime,

    the dung heaps of winter.

Quantity AND Quality?

In some utopian scheme,

Man would devise a flawless plan,

to combine these Q's of Time

and feast upon their Most and Best.

Time, forever, and with open arms,

indeed, allows the twain to join,

to walk in blissful harmony,

or suffer through a vexing union.

"Did you have a good time on your vacation?"

"Terrific! Wish it had lasted longer!"

"How much time did the Judge give Uncle Frank?"

"A hell of a lot more than Old Frank wanted."

Thus, in our thorny thickets of misery and despair,

we fuss and fret and oft forget:

Time's time allows for fun and frolic.

So, as we join the Q's of Time,

and attend the wedding feast,

simple wisdom speaks an elemental truth:

circumstance is oft-times Man's own choosing.

Thus, Time's role is not the player on the stage,

But to be the silent, faceless audience,

To watch, and wait, and watch the play unfold.

While players make their moves and speak their lines,

Time hovers quietly 'round the scene,

Proclaims no plaudits, writes no reviews.

As Man continues to search the invisible face of Time,

Seeking full measure of its Quantity and Quality,

Time will move forever and alone,

in the shadows,

silent . . . unseen . . . and unmeasured . . . . ❐

Time is the painter of Masterpieces on ugly canvas.

Time is the promise of one flickering candle;

and fullness of a light still glowing.

"…I speak of an Eternal Drumbeat."

The End

Time "Past" has passed and cannot be redeemed

> save in our bundle of memories and dreams;

Time "Present" is with us now but offers naught

> save choices, hopes and varied circumstance;

Time "Future" is yet to be, its terminus loosely fixed

> in debated prophecy and far-fetched speculation.

"The End of Time?"

> Time's ultimate dimension,
>
> proclaimed in fervid incantations,
>
> but there again,
>
> no more than the folly of fuzzy guesswork.

With all the terms and metaphors,

> that Man's mental orgies might conjure up,
>
> only one can circumscribe Time's history:
>
> that word is Time … and Time alone . . . .

Time has no plan other than to wait,

> and that eternal wait will outlive all "things,"
>
> yet offer up the promise of future things to come.

As Man's measuring devices wear down,

      the last diary,

      the last schedule of appointments,

      the noisy tenor of activity,

      all will fade.

All will fade

      into the ripple of waters not seen.

All will hush

      in the whisper of breezes not heard.

All will exit from the stage,

      leaving no hands to collect the properties.

It will surely happen.

The last sheet of the last calendar

      will somehow vanish,

      consumed by the very Time

      it was meant to record.

All the clocks,

      for reasons yet unknown,

      will stop.

Pendulums

      will hang dead still

in the monotony of silence.

The last grain of sand

will trickle through

the narrow stem of Time's hour-glass,

with no hand to turn it over.

Yes, it will ultimately be!

Even in a million centuries or so,

the recognized messengers

and recorders of Time

will be gone.

They will leave naught but questions:

Devoured by mightier predators?

If so, what happened to the predators?

Did all go in a cloud of mystery?

As did the dinosaurs?

Or were all erased by Man's erasers?

Nevertheless, they will go!

They will go as a civilization,

like other civilizations,

strong, striving civilizations,

unable to accommodate the burden of Eternity.

We,

And they,

And all,

       thus, will rest in the hollow bosom of Time.

The drumbeat of Time

       will throb to its own cadence,

       the unrecorded ticking of Time

       will go on and on and on and on and on.

Time will move quietly through

       its minutes

       and hours

       and days

       and weeks

       and months

       and years

       and centuries,

       whether or not Man

       or any living Thing

       is present to record its passing.

Time is its own substance.

Time is its own void.

All that Time needs is itself.

Through the limitless reaches of Space,

jig-sawed by the presence of Matter,

the inexorable movement of Time

will remain the silent witness,

unfettered by any worry

of its own End.

In that far reach of Time's eternal mystery,

and, somehow, through the long sleep,

there will yet be dreams.

Somewhere, flickering, in the long night of darkness,

bright visions will be a'glowing.

In the formless void, numb and senseless,

passions will be a'stirring.

And, in the grand, eternal scheme of Things and Time,

plans will evolve

for a new version

of another beginning . . . of Things.

In Time.

pendulums will again swing,

hands will turn the hour glasses,

calendars will show the schedules, and

diaries will mark the events

of new days

and months

and years

and centuries

of Time . . . .

There is no Preface to Time,

nor is there a Postscript.

Far beyond the evolving and revolving millennia of Time,

the Nagging Question:

How far ahead?

Time??

The End Will Never Be.

Time. ❐

Time is dawn and dusk and the hour of midnight.

..........The Faces

and Places

of Time..........

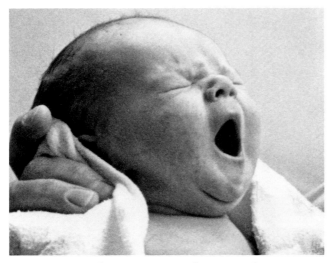

A newborn yawn at the open door

"Youth is Time's Innocent Child..."

Faces are like clocks
   that show a span of time.

Some clocks have happy faces,
   flashing bright colors
   in computed calculations.

Some clocks make merry music,
   with fine tuned chimes,
   to sound their waking calls.

Young faces, like new clocks,
   freshly polished, well-tuned...
   sentinels on the cutting edge of time.

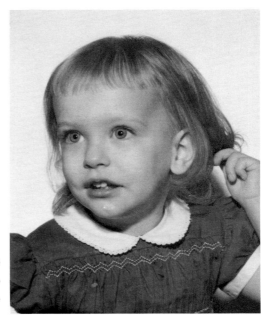

Gentle smile,
expectations,
waiting...

"Time allows for the steps of Youth…"

Autumn slumber,
warm sunshine

A nurturing soul of humankind

Probing eyes,
wide in wonderment

Bursting joy,
robust laughter

Listening for new sounds

Warm comfort,
a mother's arms

Shaded eyes,
a vast unknown

A friendly hug
on Graduation Day

The Pasture Fence

Time is a guiltless child
with innocent hopes
and smiles of expectation,
ranging far beyond
the binding reins of circumstance.

Time holds a distant echo
of promises yet unspoken,
pulsing now in happy thoughts
and eager hands that wait,
behind the pasture's fence.

"The frayed and broken threads

of memory,

weave jagged patterns

in the rags of Time."

Time is a span
that allows
reflections.

Time is a span
for laughter
and for tears.

Time is a mental journey
for Uncle Ben Turner
and spouse of sixty years.

Time, now,
is their musty scrapbook
of bittersweet memories.

Blurred Images

Youth rekindles slowly, and dimly,

Only in the blurred images of memory.

On narrow, twisting lines;

Through long and slanting shadows;

Along the ripple of still waters;

In the chorus of silent voices,

There are but vague impressions

To mark her span of Time.

Time Is An Old House

Once upon a Time,

a hundred years or so ago,

there was a sound of laughter in the house

and music from a hand-cranked phonograph.

Children scampered in their fun and games,

with dogs and cats a playful lot,

and parents gave their happy smiles

to bind the family friendships well.

All hands and voices now are gone,

likewise the laughter, fun and games;

the music box lies broken

in a barn-side wagon shed.

So now, alone, the muted subject stands,

beaten by wind and rain,

wrinkled and twisted by the sun,

eaten by worms,

and manacled by weeds and vines.

The Court of Father Time held sway,

its verdict clearly written on the Scroll:

"Mere circumstance, in Time, and Time alone,

will claim its certain toll."

The Road Forever Upward

Time is the birthplace of Expectations
and the cradle of Hope.

Time allows the open way
to search for better things.

Time provides a starting place
and the journey's end.

Time allows for brighter dreams
at a nightmare's end . . .

like a view from the hill
that looked forever downward
upon a road that looks forever upward.

Echoes Of Silent Time

Gone, the bottled linament and turpentine,

    plowshares and the sewing thread.

Gone, the hoop cheese and fatback meat,

    horse collars and the brogan shoes,

    and peppermint sticks in the candy case.

Silent now, around the stove, the talk of coming weather,

    of gossip tales, and the Preacher's Sunday sermon.

Silent now, laments of "Hoover Days," and boll weevils,

    boastings of Uncle Hank's home-made molasses,

    and hog-killing days a'coming.

Back then, and through their hours of dreaming time,

    folks heard the whistle of night trains passing,

    bemused in wonder of where their trips might end.

But now, their scattered ears and fading memories,

    sleep to the echoes of Silent Time,

    and the hollow sound of night trains passing.

Time Allows a Happy Face

Time allows mere access to the loom,
it does not weave our cloth.

A happy face is the fabric of the soul,
handwoven in the warp and woof of life.

Undaunted spirit, hearty laugh, and hope,
thus transcend misfortune and despair.

Tales No Longer Told

A fading glint of passion yet,

And fleeting thoughts of youthful revelry,

Alive, but hanging threadbare now,

Only in the frayed fringes of memory.

Thus, Time's decree is firm and fixed,

Deaf to the plaintive plea,

It rules that man cannot go back

To where the boy has been.

But yet, there is a drumbeat in the soul,

Faint echoes pulse the anxious heartstrings,

The mind still stirs in ageing recollections,

Through the book of tales no longer told.

Time Allows For Planting Oats

Squire Jennings still "felt his oats,"
the townfolks said,
at a perky eighty-seven.

And, rightly so, most all agreed,
he had planted quite a bag full,
and the good ones grew to harvest.

He owned, outright, the general store,
some land, a warm cigar,
an easy chair, a gold chain on his watch,
a walking stick of sturdy stuff,
and a modest bank account.

Times had, indeed, been good,
the Squire acknowledged,
as he smiled, spun yarns and reminisced,
and combed the sturdy threads of memory.

The Sound Of Cold Wind Blowing

No sounds of song and laughter,

No touch of hands,

No warming smiles,

There is no smell of baking bread,

No scampering, playful kitten.

Long furrows and a fallow field

Are now untended

By the tiller's hand.

The house is cold,

The floors are bare,

The winter sun slants through a broken door.

Time breathes but a single sound

Of cold wind whining

    through open cracks

    and shattered window panes;

There is but the single sound

Of cold wind blowing.

Time Is A Distant Drumbeat

Young soldiers passing on parade,

    with marching bands and flags unfurled,

    the First World War was done.

One stood alone in proud salute,

    his hand across his breast,

    but heard a distant swelling sound

    from another place and time.

He heard the sound of cannon fire,

    along the ridgetop over there;

He heard the sound of bugles calling,

    and the distant thump of drumbeats.

He heard again that certain call to duty,

    the Time to muster up,

    and face-off brothers Blue and Gray.

The Old Soldier now, in Time, is gone,

    the colors blue and gray have blended some,

    and across their once-stained battlefields,

    the poppies bloom and grasses grow.

Time Hit Rock Bottom

With little more

than hope and time,

from a swirling storm of dust,

to sunshine and lush green fields,

in a far-off promised land.

Stalled and stranded by circumstance,

in the ditch and out of gas.

"My Old Lady here beside me,"

he said,

"And seven younguns in the back."

Hard times, for Luther Williford,

from the State of Oklahoma,

"Ain't too far,"

he said,

"from hittin' rock bottom."

Honed By The Cutting Edge Of Time

Old Sam was eighty-three, he said,

      but had never learned to frown,

      or feel bad about himself.

Sam, of tattered hat and calloused hands,

      always whistled while he worked,

      and he did a lot of both.

Sam, of unsophisticated notions,

      never looked back, but seemed to know

      that Time was "catching up."

Sam stoutly bore the abrasions of Time,

      with a simple sense of pride,

      and somewhere must be smiling yet.

Time Has A Happy Face

Time is good humor
between the miseries.

Time is hearty laughter
between the tears.

Time has a happy face
on a Saturday night
at the Medicine Show
when Doctor Constantine
peddles his bottles of cure-all
and tells funny jokes.

Miseries and tears,
if any, and if ever,
are put aside
on a Saturday night,
while the Medicine Man
tells funny jokes.

A Face Of Time

History is written on the face of Time,

Yet Time, itself, deserves no scolding

For the ominous images mirrored by

The auction blocks of human bondage.

Time earns no guilt for Man's misdeeds,

Nor bears his pain and scars of Age.

Time speaks no words of calumny or of praise,

Time pays no penalties, reaps no rewards.

    As Mankind sequesters in the jury room,

    Time stands alone without judicial garb,

    Cast forever as a silent, moving witness,

    Awaiting - and always now - the verdict.

Scar Marks Of Time

The face bore scar marks

of a love long lost;

the eyes were locked in a haunting search

for passions unrewarded;

tight lips showed no zeal to speak

of future searches or of reasons.

A huddled mass of vanquished hope,

etched by the abrasions of Time,

shouldering now the crushing burden,

a heavy bundle of broken dreams.

Hard Times With A Smile

Migrant worker,

    widow,

    mother of five,

    in the summer of 'thirty-three,

    waiting for beans to mature.

Caught in a cycle of Time,

    and the web of circumstance,

    leaning on naught

    but self-whispered words

    of hope and promise.

Time, alone, and nurturing that thought,

    outlives every human condition,

    and speaks that silent truth

    for all who dare to smile

    while bean fields grow to harvest.

Time's Fleeting Smile

There was a hole in the bag

      she carried her joys in,

      they were strewn and lost along the way.

      tomorrows come, tomorrows come . . . tomorrow,

      but all her smiles were in yesterdays.

So much the joys, so brief their stay,

      so far did her eager strivings roam,

      so strong the laboring heart searched on,

      searched on, and on.

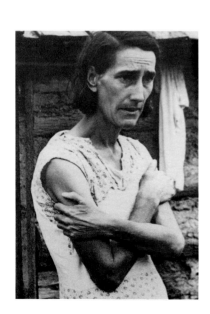

But circumstances bore no threads

      to mend the broken bag,

      or willing hands to join the search

      for one simple joy long lost.

So now, in evening time and slanting shadows,

      memory probes the scraps of Time's old rubbish pile,

      with hope to catch one brief and happy glimpse

      of Time's last fleeting smile.

Time At Aunt Carrie's

The younger folks used to say

that Aunt Carrie's place looked pretty sad.

But, Aunt Carrie would always declare:

"Well now, I guess it ain't too bad."

"I raised nine children here," she said,

"And mended, cooked, and washed the clothes,"

("with wash tub, lye soap, and a scrubbing
board,"

she always liked to add.)

"My Old Man was always good to me,

the Younguns all made it through,

and I'm ninety-one and feeling pretty good,

what else do you reckon I could do?"

Youth, it is often claimed,

is Time's innocent child.

Age, it is often charged,

is Time's visible guilt.

Time is Youth and Age and Circumstance,

meshed and blended into images reflected;

Time's ultimate gift is one single promise,

and Aunt Carrie discovered its beauty.

Holes And Scars

No glittering trips
       on sailing ships,
No airline whirls
       around the world,
No grand adventure
       to foreign shores.

Her measured pathways travelled
       were never long,
       the tedium of a narrow way,
       bounded by dreary circumstance.

Around in circles,
       a hard and dusty yard;
To and from
       long rows of rock and clod,
       through planting times,
       through tending times,
       through harvest times.

Down a rutted road
       to spring and stream,
       water buckets to fill,
       and carry up the hill,
       for cooking time
       and washing time.

The long and fruitless journey
       bore no lasting joys;
       the stockings and the feet
       were worn and bruised,
       with only holes to prove the scars.

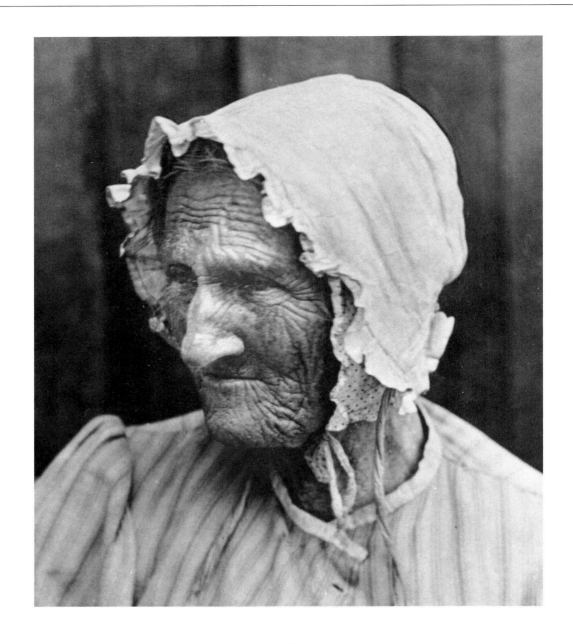

Time Past

So distant now,

and long ago,

it seems,

like the jagged edge

of a broken dream.

Ashes Of Youth

Age is the ashes of youth,

the fading embers,

the cooling hearth.

Time is the silent witness,

watching the thin grey smoke

swirling into oblivion.

A Leaf Grown Old

Time is a leaf grown old,
Whose autumn day has come,
Time's frost has turned its edges brown,
It's wrinkled in the sun.

Its withered stem of life is broke,
The limb has cast it down,
To nourish with its crumpled frame,
Another Springtime tree.

Rattling Leaves

Time is rattling the leaves again,

    that's just the way it is,

    this time of year.

Time's icy finger is the villain,

    stroking these tiny, fragile things,

    with dry cold fury.

It's Autumn-Time.

    Time's time for old spent leaves

    to rattle like old bones,

    wrinkle like old faces,

    curl up like frail fingers,

    and fall down like halting feet.

It's Autumn-Time,

    and time for old, cold leaves to rattle.

Swelling Buds

Time is swelling the buds again,

    that's just the way it is,

    this time of year.

Time, with its helpmate, Nature,

    is warming and watering the growing things,

    with the Mother's gentle touch.

It's Spring-Time.

    Time for the bud to swell,

    like a pregnant womb,

    giving birth to a welcome blossom,

    as Nature fulfills its promise.

It's Spring-Time!

    and Time for young buds to bloom.

Time Allows Itself Time To Be Funny

No need to ask
that age-old question!!

The answer is "Neither."

Before the chicken,
before the egg,
before man,
woman and babies,
before all living, growing
and multiplying things . . . .

Time was.

Time laid the egg;

Time hatched the chicken;

or Vice Versa.

Time, alone, is a blank span of endless dimensions.
Time's only tool is Mother Nature,
with her own blueprints and her own commands.
Thus, Time earns no praise for the Beauty of all creation.
Time deserves no blame for Blemishes that Nature renders.

Nature's Beauty

Beauty sleeps on the mountain,
and on the Mirror of the Lake,
for a day, for a year,
for a century, a millenium, or longer,
while Nature adorns her garment.

Nature's Blemish

Blemish explodes in nightmare,

the Earth erupts, the boiling caldron flows.

Beauty's code is broken when Nature shreds her garment.

The Tools of Time at Work Again

Beauty spreads her paint on Nature's canvas,
                      hanging icicles on granite boulders
                                    like glittering shards of crystal.

Sprinkling

snowflakes,

clinging

soft,

like

Winter's

blanket.

Beauty then blows

her warming breath,

ices thaw, and

timid streams

begin to trickle,

until, in Time, the

bolder waters fall.

Winter's melting spoils

and Springtime rains:

Time's sculpting tool,

deft Nature strokes,

then gouge the clay

and flush the wounds.

At times, in a burst of Nature's seeming wrath, flood waters roll as Beauty yields to Blemish.

Invisible, sterile...Time moves on...in ageless stride...as Blemish heals...
and Beauty smiles again. Time, mute Time...an innocent witness...
beyond all words...of praise or scorn...from those of Beauty or of Blemish....

Steps To Nowhere

Time does not walk with us,
     to hold our hands or guide our way;
     it only marks our starting place,
     and awaits the journey's end.

Time does not plant roses by our path,
     or clutter it with thorns;
     it only allows the seeds we sow,
     that on the whims of nature grow.

Time is thus no more than steps
     that do not move;
     like steps in time,
     that lead to nowhere.

Twin Monuments

Time is a monument to skill,
        and to caring, calloused hands,
        that fit each stone in place,
        and stroked each binding joint.

Time is now the lonely guardian,
        listening to the echoes
        of the hammer and the trowel,
        and the sound of workmen singing.

Thus, Time could do no more
        than offer up its vacant self,
        to the hands of willing labor,
        as they raised their sturdy monument.

England's Time

On a narrow, twisting lane of England's Time,
stone fences and rows of hedge around,
some farmer marked this his hallowed spot,
and left his prints upon this ancient ground.

Gone now his happy voice and sturdy countenance,
covered with the clods that bore him then,
where is he now who tilled these fields?
where is the plow his hands did tend?

Another Springtime

There are ashes on the hearth,

the embers are cooling,

the last spark wiggles into darkness.

That is Time at work,

chilling warm passions of Youth,

stealing treasured memories of the heart.

Yet Time allows a restless yearning,

sifting through the scraps of Winter,

seeking fresh flowers for another Springtime.

Time And Shoveling Snow

Shoveling snow,
        like casting seeds,
        or mowing hay,
        or raking leaves.

Swirling seasons,
        rushing through each other,
        like hurried lives
        that come and go, like shoveling snow.

Time: A Youngster's Challenge

It's like being early, but not too soon;

Or being tardy, but not too late.

It's like now, the present, at this moment;

Not in the past, or yet too far ahead.

Seize it, hold it, embrace it,

Say something to it.

    Whisper, mumble, or shout it,

    wring your hands, shift your feet.

Proclaim It! Say it,

    if but unto yourself alone:

    "This! This is my Time."

Time's Little Sermon

Not long ago,

one friend, well educated and intended,

said to another:

    "You will not live forever."

    "Oh?!" responded the other,

    in a bold, exclamatory question,

    "Who told you so?"

    "That's just the way it is," the first one said.

    "And, what about you?" the second one asked.

    "I'm working on it," came the answer, with a smile.

Time's Gold Dust

Upon a hill

    above Bonanza Creek,

    crude wooden crosses

    mark the spots

    where miners put

    their shovels down.

Gone now the finders

    and the seekers too,

    their fortunes squandered

    or never found.

In Time

    the gold dust blows away,

    the wooden crosses fall and rot,

    but there green grasses grow,

    and fragrant flowers bloom.

Time And A Funeral

We mark these mourners yet among the living,

rich vibrant souls, awake,

and searching out life's golden promise.

But yet, how soon these marks will fade,

and Time will wash the pages blank . . .

until, and somewhere, along the way,

through Time's eternal span,

some hand shall write it all again.

The Chisel

Time is the chisel

that cut the dates and deeds

upon this ancient stone.

Time's cutting tools will grind away,

until some distant age,

when the stone itself is gone.

Then, when all have long forgotten,

and across the barren sands,

the lettered dates and deeds,

will blow and shift on the silent winds.

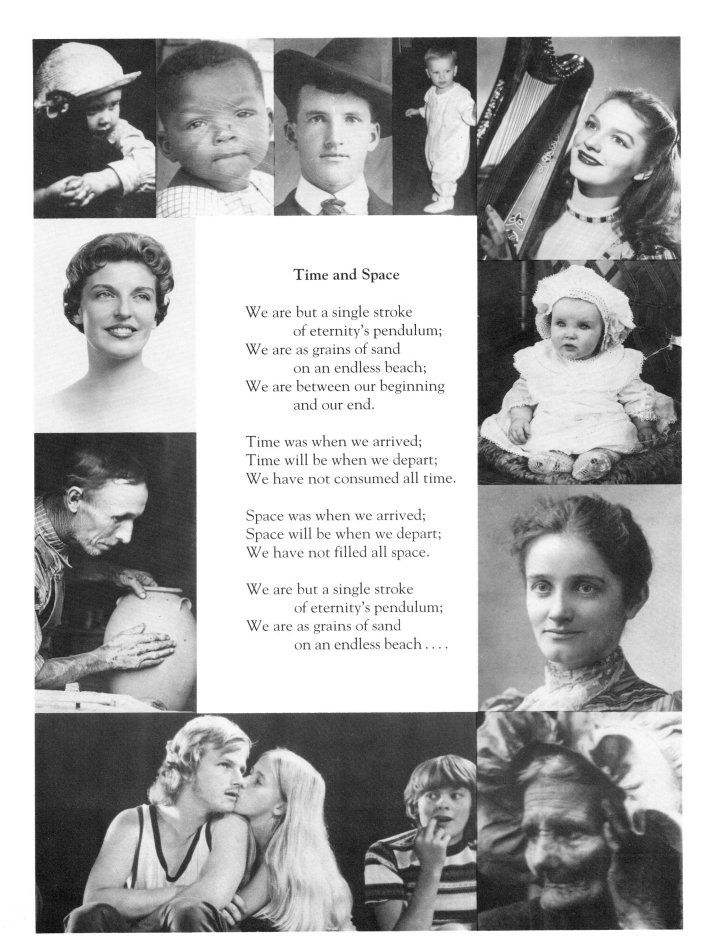

Time and Space

We are but a single stroke
       of eternity's pendulum;
We are as grains of sand
       on an endless beach;
We are between our beginning
       and our end.

Time was when we arrived;
Time will be when we depart;
We have not consumed all time.

Space was when we arrived;
Space will be when we depart;
We have not filled all space.

We are but a single stroke
       of eternity's pendulum;
We are as grains of sand
       on an endless beach . . . .

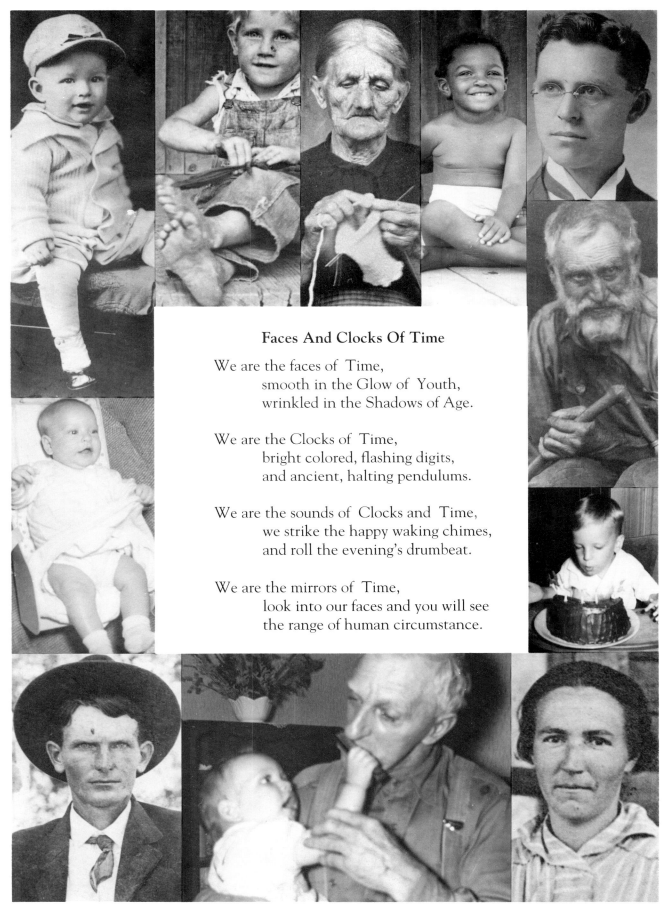

Faces And Clocks Of Time

We are the faces of Time,
       smooth in the Glow of Youth,
       wrinkled in the Shadows of Age.

We are the Clocks of Time,
       bright colored, flashing digits,
       and ancient, halting pendulums.

We are the sounds of Clocks and Time,
       we strike the happy waking chimes,
       and roll the evening's drumbeat.

We are the mirrors of Time,
       look into our faces and you will see
       the range of human circumstance.

Time . . . The End . . . ? . . . ? . . . ? . . .

In Eternity's span of Future Time,
   whether by an aberrant whim of nature,
   misguided steps in Man's behavior,
   or a cycle of Providential Promise,
   all things will be uprooted and rearranged.

Immovables will be moved,
   boulders will glow like fiery embers,
   molten ruins will flow as raging rivers,
   gasses will range with strange new winds,
   as waters gouge uncharted courses . . . .

" . . . misguided steps in Man's behavior . . . "

84

Somewhere, in a reassembled Universe,
　　new worlds will come to order,
　　fresh minds will probe leftover clues,
　　blank pages will be spread
　　for speculation scribes of ancient history.

As Time thus honors
　　its eternal but unspoken promise,
　　new things will be,
　　new light will shine,
　　and there will yet be heartbeats.

"...or a cycle of Providential Promise..."

Picture Credits

Picture Credits (continued)

Frame Number	Source
1	Barnhill Collection Mars Hill College
2	Library of Congress
3, 5, 7, 8, 9	Mars Hill College
10	George Dunkle, Potter Barnhill Collection Mars Hill College
4, 6, 11	Scrapbook

Page 82 layout:

```
| 1 | 2 | 3 | 4 | 5 |
| 11 |        | 6 |
|    | Time   |
| 10 | and    | 7 |
|    | Space  |
|    9        | 8 |
```

Page 83

Frame Number	Source
1, 5, 6	Mars Hill College #1, Lunsford Collection #6, Ulman Collection
2, 4	Library of Congress
3	Barnhill Collection Pack Memorial Library, Asheville, NC
7, 8, 9, 10, 11	Scrapbook

Page 83 layout:

```
| 1 | 2 | 3 | 4 | 5 |
|   |        |   | 6 |
|   | Faces  |   |
|   | and    |   |
| 11| Clocks |   | 7 |
|   | Of Time|   |
| 10|   9        | 8 |
```

It's A Matter of Time . . . .

is available by mail.

Cost Per Copy	$ 20.00
N. C. Sales Tax @ 6%	1.20
Shipping & Handling (one copy)	3.00
(Two or more copies, $ 2.00 each)	

Please send <u>Name</u>, <u>Mailing Address</u>, <u>Zip Code</u> & <u>Telephone Number</u>

To: Carolina Heritage Press
P. O. Box 669
Shelby, NC 28150
(704) 487-4583

Include check or money order, payable to Carolina Heritage Press.
—Allow four weeks for delivery—

<u>Also Available:</u>

(S.C. Sales
Tax, 5%)

White House Inn
607 West Pine Street
Blacksburg, South Carolina 29702
(803)839-3000

A First Edition Printing of 1,000 copies will be numbered and signed.

A sum of $10.00 from the sale of each book will be applied to a $10,000 Endowed Scholarship Fund recently established at the Shelby (NC) High School to assist qualified and deserving students in continuing their education.

It is my purpose, and hope, that annual grants from this Fund will motivate more young people to develop keener interests in government, public service, and the political process.

It is my further hope that the Scholarship's criteria will challenge students to consider long term commitments to active personal involvements in addressing these critical issues.

Lester D. Roark

(Comments Welcome; mail to: P. O. Box 669, Shelby, NC 28150)

time
time
time
time
time
time
time
time
time
time
time
time
time
time
time
time
time
time
time
time
time
time
time
time
time
time
time
time
time
time
time
time
time
time
time
time
time
time
time
time
time
time
time
time
time
time
time
time
time
time
time
tim
time
time
time
time
time
time
time
time
time

Time is the forge and the factory to build new Universes.